Myth Quest

Narasimha

THE GREAT PROTECTOR

retold by Anu Kumar

illustrations by Maya Magical Studios

First published in 2012 by Hachette India
(Registered name: Hachette Book Publishing India Pvt. Ltd)
An Hachette UK company
www.hachetteindia.com

SRD

ISBN 978-93-5009-324-5

Hachette Book Publishing India Pvt Ltd,
4th & 5th Floors, Corporate Centre;
Plot No. 94, Sector 44; Gurgaon 122003, India

Typeset in Adobe Garamond Pro 13/16
by Eleven Arts, New Delhi

Printed and bound in India by
Manipal Technologies Limited, Manipal

Welcome to the world of MythQuest . . .

Discover the fables and legends about the origin, history, deities, ancestors and heroes of India.

While the term 'myth' in common conversation means a false story, in the world of religion, folklore and magic, myths are considered 'true'. They tell stories of the creation of the universe, the eternal battle between good and evil and the history of humankind itself.

The main characters in our myths are bigger and better than any modern superheroes. They are birds and beasts, gods and demons, kings and queens, generals and warriors, sages and gurus, each with extraordinary powers that changed the course of history and the fate of the human race.

The people to whom a myth belongs consider it a true account of their past millions of years ago. Even today, they continue to worship the gods and goddesses, follow the rituals and read the texts that developed from these myths.

Hachette India's MythQuest series brings to you fascinating stories from the vast treasures of ancient mythology. Read them all—and become a MythMaster!

Mythological characters and events have been described in different ways in different versions of ancient texts. We have chosen the most interesting and key stories to build a comprehensive account for the young reader.

This story is about . . .

. . . Narasimha, half-man and half-lion, fearsome and ferocious in every aspect, and yet protector to those in need. An incarnation of Lord Vishnu, the Preserver of the Universe, Narasimha represents his divine anger. Lord Vishnu took on this fearsome avatar to slay an evil demon and the Narasimha avatar has been venerated since as a destroyer of evil.

Narasimha is shown as an awe-inspiring figure with the head and claws of a lion and the body of a man. He is sometimes shown with 16 arms, two of which hold the conch and the chakra, *and three others are seen disembowelling the wicked demon Hiranyakashipu.*

He is referred to in the Bhagavata Purana, the Agni Purana, the Vayu Purana, the Kurma Purana, the Brahma Purana and the Linga Purana, among others. Narasimha has nine forms (Nava Narasimha) based on the different postures and weapons that he wields.

Despite his awe-inspiring image and powers, Lord Narasimha is worshipped because he is a reminder of how Lord Vishnu appears from time to time to alleviate the sufferings of devotees, save the universe and ensure its continuity in the face of dire threats. As the 'Great Protector', Narasimha is a popular deity and there are ancient temples in western and southern India dedicated to this god.

Read about Narasimha's great victories, sometimes glorious, sometimes bloody and always thrilling . . .

CHAPTER ONE

HOW THE PILLAR CRACKED FROM SIDE TO SIDE

Our story begins in the middle of the action. The universe was being ravaged by *asuras* and they had never been more powerful. Led by their evil king Hiranyakashipu, they plagued the gods and humans alike. Hiranyakashipu had always hated Vishnu. He blamed Vishnu for having killed his brother Hiranyaksha and now he was out for revenge. As king of the *asuras*, he had the power to wreak great havoc. He instructed his soldiers to destroy every image of

Vishnu and to torment and kill all those who persisted in worshipping Vishnu. The *asura* army went on a rampage and destroyed temples and idols all over the world and killed many of Lord Vishnu's devotees.

However, they missed one of Lord Vishnu's greatest devotees who was no other than Hiranyakashipu's son, Prahlada. He was as unlike his father as water from oil. He tried to pull his father away from the evil path that he was bent upon following. But all his entreaties fell on deaf ears as Hiranyakashipu believed he was all-powerful and invincible, and even better than the gods.

One day, Prahlada went up to his father in a last-ditch attempt to make him see the error of his ways. 'Father, please give up your wrongful ways,' said Prahlada, folding his hands in respect. 'If you beg for Lord Vishnu's forgiveness, I am sure he will show mercy and forgive you immediately. You can still be as powerful as you are, but along with that you will also be deeply loved and admired by all. No one will fear you, or feel terrorized by you; instead they will look up to you and sing your praises.'

Hiranyakashipu bristled at the mere mention of Lord Vishnu. With a laugh, he mocked his son's words. 'Will your great Lord Vishnu come to your rescue if I decide to harm you?' He then preened before his son, telling him how he had defeated the gods themselves and become the supreme overlord of the universe. He poked fun at the defeated gods who had rushed to Vaikuntha—the abode of Lord Vishnu—to seek his protection.

'Is he going to protect you, just as he is protecting the gods?' he said with a malicious laugh. His guffaws resounded around his entire palace, while the pillars shook and the very earth trembled at its sound.

All the other people in the palace shuddered in fear, but Prahlada remained calm and collected as he continued to speak. 'Father, you may be a mighty king, but Lord Vishnu is far greater than you can imagine. It is he who has given me the courage to speak up against your heinous ways. He is stronger than anyone else. You and I, the universe, and no other god, can match him in strength and power. He is the Supreme Lord of the Universe, the Great Preserver, and he is present everywhere.'

Hiranyakashipu stopped laughing for a minute and pointed to a nearby pillar. 'Is that so? Is Lord Vishnu present in that stone pillar behind you?'

Prahlada repeated what he had said before, and added, 'Yes, he exists in the pillar and in the smallest leaf and the humblest twig.'

Hiranyakashipu's laughter turned to rage at his son's words. Roaring with anger, Hiranyakashipu smashed the pillar with a single powerful blow of his mace.

Almost immediately, cracks opened across the pillar. There was an ear-splitting sound as if the universe itself had split into two. Even the very confident Hiranyakashipu looked momentarily startled at the deafening boom coming from the stone pillar.

The courtiers froze in fear and turned into mute statues, unable to stir, or utter a sound. And as they looked on, the cracks widened with a great rumble and the pillar split into two.

Everyone in Hiranyakashipu's court including the great *asura* king and his son Prahlada, waited with bated breath to see what would happen next. Just as the dust and debris from the cracked pillar settled, there was a great gust of fire and smoke, and a fearsome sight greeted all who were present . . .

CHAPTER TWO

THE TERRIBLE DEATH OF HIRANYAKASHIPU

A shadow moved within the pillar. As some light fell on it, people could make out its shape and it was the strangest creature they had ever seen. It was a great fire-breathing monster, with a flaming yellow mane. It had a lion's head and a lion's claws, and the tawny, hairy body of a man.

The *asuras* quaked in fear as they recognized what they beheld. For this was no other than the great Narasimha. Ancient prophecies had foretold the arrival of this Vishnu avatar when danger threatened to outweigh all the goodness in this universe.

Narasimha's eyes were a fiery yellow and gleamed

like molten gold. In fact, his very complexion glowed with a golden sheen. His many arms were thickly muscled and his claws ended in piercing long nails. Narasimha's mane, his moustache and beard stood straight and erect. His jaws were pointed and the tongue was like a fine point of an arrow. He emitted a roar that equalled the sound of a thousand swords slicing up the sky. His shaggy eyebrows were close-knit and furrowed. The ears were cocked straight up at the sky and his mouth hung open like a giant mountain cave.

Never before had anyone seen such a gigantic and terrifying creature. He kept growing in size until his head touched the high ceiling of Hiranyakashipu's lofty palace. The remnants of the pillar fell to the floor with a resounding crash as Narasimha, fully formed, stepped out.

Hiranyakashipu's courtiers had crowded the hall; but not one dared to look at Narasimha as he moved towards them. They stood rooted to the ground and trembled in fear. Only Hiranyakashipu did not flinch, for despite all his faults, the *asura* king was indeed extraordinarily courageous. He looked Narasimha in the eye steadily for he understood what was going to happen.

'Oh, so this is Lord Vishnu himself, come to see me in person. And this is the same god who killed my brother in the form of a wild boar,' he muttered. 'If I kill him today, all the gods will be completely helpless;

they will be like the branches of a tree whose trunk has been forever torn asunder. Well, I shall test his strength or at least die trying.'

Hiranyakashipu then raised his mace and fell upon Narasimha. Although Hiranyakashipu was a man of great strength, he was rendered powerless against Narasimha whose size seemed to grow with every passing moment. He seized Hiranyakashipu as easily as Garuda, the great bird-king, would seize a little serpent.

However, the *asura* king managed to wriggle away from his grip.

Narasimha caught him again like a snake seizing a mouse; this time, the great *asura* was helpless and couldn't free himself despite his best efforts. With a loud roar, the great creature carried Hiranyakashipu to the threshold of the palace hall. There he sat, right on the doorway, with the *asura* placed across his lap like a limp puppet. Then, he dug his nails deep into the *asura*'s body and ripped it open.

And before the horrified eyes of everyone watching, Narasimha proceeded to tear Hiranyakashipu's body bit by bit and devoured him completely. Thus, the wicked *asura* met a bloody end at the hands of the half-man, half-lion—Narasimha—who was an avatar of the very god the *asura* had mocked so foolishly.

CHAPTER THREE

NARASIMHA'S ANGER

Now Vishnu appeared in the form of Narasimha because he had promised the gods that he would intervene to rid the universe of the menace of Hiranyakashipu. He had to assume such a form because Hiranyakashipu had been clever and had performed severe penances for Lord Brahma, the Creator of the Universe. Pleased with his efforts, the god had appeared before him and granted him the boon he had asked for.

Hiranyakashipu asked for death at the hands of a creature who was not born of Brahma, the Creator. He asked for death in a location that was neither within a house nor outside it. He asked for death at a time of day when it was neither day, nor night. He asked for death in a place that was neither on the earth, nor in the sky. He asked for death that was neither at the hands of an animal, a weapon, a human being, a demigod, a demon, nor by any great snake from *patala*. As Brahma granted him this boon, Hiranyakashipu became nearly immortal and presided over demons, humans, gods and all the other creatures of the universe.

So when the time came for Lord Vishnu to destroy him, he had to make sure he did so without violating any of the boons the *asura* had received from Lord Brahma. Thus was born Narasimha, who was not a creature created by Lord Brahma, but an avatar of Lord Vishnu himself. Lord Vishnu as the Preserver, along with Lord Brahma and Lord Shiva, the Destroyer of the Universe, were eternal, and thus, also unborn.

Narasimha came to life when the *asura*, in his arrogance, kicked at a stone pillar.

He then proceeded to overcome and carry Hiranyakashipu to the threshold of the latter's palace and kill him. So he was killed in a spot that was neither within his residence nor outside it, as Brahma had ordained. The time of his death was the twilight hour, and so it was neither day nor night.

Narasimha placed him across his lap, so he was neither on the ground, nor in the sky. Besides, he was a creature like no other, a half-man and a half-lion, and so Brahma's boon that Hiranyakashipu could not be killed by either a human, or a weapon, or an animal was not contradicted. Narasimha used his claws to rip Hiranyakashipu apart, and claws did not count as weapons. And so every single stipulation of the boon was met, and Hiranyakashipu was finally killed.

As Narasimha sat calmly devouring the *asura* who had so long tormented the universe, Hiranyakashipu's bodyguards and the other courtiers stood speechless and motionless in fear. But in no time, they sprang to action. In a fierce rage, they fell on Narasimha as one united body. But they were all crushed in the wink of an eye.

After the enemies had been destroyed, Narasimha sat on Hiranyakashipu's former throne from where the latter had lorded over the universe. The gods showered flowers from heaven. The demigods sang divine songs and the *apsaras* danced in joy. The entire universe rejoiced with them.

However, the terrible anger of Narasimha continued unabated. Even Goddess Lakshmi, Lord Vishnu's consort, was afraid to go near him, to appease his fierce rage.

It was then that Prahlada walked up and bowed low before Narasimha. Being a devotee of Lord Vishnu, he knew without a doubt that this was his favourite god in one of his incarnations. Pleased by Prahlada's devotion,

Narasimha grew calmer and his rage gave way to gentleness. He then got up and placed Prahlada on the throne and pronounced him the king of the *asuras*.

In tears, Prahlada asked Narasimha about the fate that would befall his father after his death. Narasimha then reminded Prahlada of the curse of the Kumaras and assured his devotee that as his father had been killed by Lord Vishnu himself and had shown great courage, he would surely return to Vaikuntha one day. Narasimha also promised Prahlada that henceforth, no one from his dynasty would die at the hands of Lord Vishnu.

The universe was finally at peace after Hiranyakashipu had been killed. But things had not always been like this and Hiranyakashipu wasn't always evil. Like many random acts in the universe, the whole thing was a result of a terrible curse that had transformed the faithful gatekeepers of Lord Vishnu into the deeply feared *asura* brothers—Hiranyaksha and Hiranyakashipu.

CHAPTER FOUR

THE CURSE OF THE KUMARAS

The two *asura* brothers Hiranyaksha and Hiranyakashipu were originally divine beings called Jaya and Vijaya, and they had for long been gatekeepers to Vishnu's abode—Vaikuntha—which rested on the coils of the eternal snake, Sheshanaga.

Both Jaya and Vijaya loved Lord Vishnu fiercely and were his loyal gatekeepers. Like many other heavenly beings, they were blessed with the gift of immortality. However, all of this was doomed to change the day they were cursed by the Kumaras.

This happened when they refused entry to the four Kumaras, who were great sages born from Lord Brahma's concentration. The Kumaras were all born at the same time and resembled each other. Although they were tiny and looked like little children, they were actually very powerful sages who had spent years in meditation and had acquired immense powers. Their names were Sanaka, Sanandana, Sanatana and Sanatkumara, and having spent long years in meditation, they came to Vaikuntha to pay their respects to Lord Vishnu and his consort, Goddess Lakshmi.

The Kumaras travelled a long, hard way across the universe to finally reach Vaikuntha, which was quite secluded. As they approached the gate and were about to enter, they were stopped by Jaya and Vijaya, who were fearsome to look at and imposing in size.

'Halt! Where do you think you are going?' they boomed. 'You are small children and you cannot enter sacred Vaikuntha so casually and disturb its peace and tranquillity with your chatter.'

One of the Kumaras tried to explain matters to them patiently and reveal their true identity, but Jaya and Vijaya could be fairly stubborn and refused to listen to a word they were saying. They were fiercely protective of Lord Vishnu, and his comfort and safety was foremost on their minds at all times. They told the Kumaras that it was already very late—Lord Vishnu was resting and could not be disturbed at any cost. Jaya and Vijaya's brutish behaviour began to irk the Kumaras and despite their efforts to stay calm, they started to get angry.

One of them testily responded that Vishnu was available to his devotees any time and he never let them down especially if they wanted to see him desperately. But Jaya and Vijaya would not yield. They could be very stubborn, and so the four Kumaras in unison pronounced a curse on them: 'For your stubbornness and your unwillingness to unbend, O vain gatekeepers, you will lose your divinity. You will be born on earth, and live like those normal humans, who have to struggle and toil every day and live in fear of death and the vain hope for redemption.'

These words were uttered in loud and severe tones as the Kumaras were indeed very angry. They were so loud that even Lord Vishnu heard every word that was uttered. He also heard the loud protestations on the part of Jaya and Vijaya. Knowing he had to intervene, Lord Vishnu appeared just when things started to get even more heated up.

Jaya and Vijaya looked most contrite and relieved as he appeared. Together, they appealed to him to undo the curse of the Kumaras. But Lord Vishnu shook his head. The little sages had been blessed with great powers that they had acquired through long, rigorous years of meditation. Their curse could not be revoked so easily.

But then again Jaya and Vijaya had been such faithful and loyal gatekeepers and had protected him with such devotion, that Vishnu could not let them bear this difficult curse without any hope. He offered the brothers two options.

The first option was to take seven births on earth as devotees of Vishnu, and the second was to be born three successive times as his staunchest, bitterest enemies who would stoop to no ends to humiliate him.

After serving either of these sentences, Jaya and Vijaya would easily regain their divine stature and return to Vaikuntha and be with him permanently. To help them further, Vishnu also promised that he would intervene and appear in one incarnation or another to release them from their curse.

Jaya and Vijaya could not bear the thought of staying away from Vishnu for seven consecutive lives, even if they spent their days in a virtuous manner. So they chose the second option where they would be born three times on earth even though it would have to be as enemies of Lord Vishnu, and thus they would end their punishment sooner.

That is how Jaya and Vijaya were born as the evil *asuras* Hiranyakashipu and Hiranyaksha in their first life. In accordance with the curse of the Kumaras, they were sworn enemies of Lord Vishnu and kept trying to come up with ways to thwart the great Preserver of the Universe. Holding to his promise, Vishnu also appeared on earth in two very fierce incarnations—once as a fearsome boar, Varaha, and then as Narasimha to kill the *asura* brothers and end their cursed existence.

In their second life, Jaya and Vijaya were born as the feared *rakshasa* brothers, Ravana, the evil king of Lanka, and his equally terrifying brother, Kumbhakarna. They were defeated by Rama, who was an incarnation of Vishnu and the story of this battle is narrated in the Ramayana. Finally, in their third rebirth, Jaya and Vijaya were born as Shishupala, the wicked king of Chedi who was Krishna's cousin, and Dantavakra, the evil king of Karusha who was Shishupala's great friend. They were killed by Krishna, yet another powerful Vishnu avatar and the story of their defeat and death is recounted in the Mahabharata.

CHAPTER FIVE

THE TALE OF THE ASURA BROTHERS

When the time arrived for the curse to come true, Jaya and Vijaya were born to Diti and Kashyapa, as the *asuras* Hiranyaksha and Hiranyakashipu, along with all the *asuras* in the universe. They also had a sister, the demoness Holika.

Diti was one of Kashyapa's several wives. She gave birth to the *asuras*, while her sister Aditi became the mother of all the gods. Diti was usually mean and cruel to her sister and obsessed with trying to elevate the power of *asuras*. She would constantly pester her husband, the sage Kashyapa to work miracles so that the *asuras* became strong and invincible, especially against the gods. For Diti could not bear her sons to be second best, and that is why she hated Aditi's sons, who were gods and were blessed with various gifts including that of immortality.

Hiranyaksha and Hiranyakashipu, egged on by their mother, grew up to be the bitterest enemies of the gods. They were always waging war against them. Everything the gods stood for—truth, goodness and the right path, the *asuras* opposed. The *asuras* were also intensely jealous of all the happiness and the comforts the gods enjoyed in Heaven, and were always plotting to oust them from

there. They were also really shrewd and performed many austerities and propitiated many gods—and in the course of time, they gained limitless powers that they used for their own ends and for unleashing evil.

Hiranyaksha, whose name means 'golden-eyed', was younger, but in a short span, he managed to let loose great terror on Heaven and on earth too.

The gods appealed to Lord Vishnu for help, while the sages and holy men spent days in meditation, hoping for an end to their ordeal. When Hiranyaksha had terrorized the universe and no one was spared his atrocities, Lord Vishnu decided to intervene, especially after the *asura* stole the earth from its place in the skies and hid it deep inside the universal ocean.

He took on the form of a white boar, or his Varaha avatar, and appeared on earth. He came face to face with Hiranyaksha and battled with him for a thousand years. Finally, with one swipe of his powerful snout, Lord Vishnu as Varaha, killed the evil *asura*. Then diving deep into the cosmic ocean, the great Preserver pulled the earth out from the darkest depths, where Hiranyaksha had hidden it away. Varaha carried the earth carefully on his snout and restored it to its rightful place in the universe.

At the death of Hiranyaksha, his wife Vrishadbhanu and their children were overcome with grief. Hiranyaksha's mother, Diti, was especially heart-broken and longed for revenge. Hiranyakashipu for his part was consumed by a raging anger when he learnt of how Vishnu had

killed his brother. Hiranyakashipu resolved to avenge his brother's death by any means possible.

Vishnu's name now became like poison to him and Hiranyakashipu's blood boiled with hatred towards the god. He called the generals of his army, Illyala, Namuchi and others, and ordered, 'Give the devotees of Vishnu as much trouble as you can. Make them realize that the god whom they worship with such adoration is in fact powerless against me and can do nothing to protect them.'

And so Hiranyakashipu's men went on a rampage, burning cities, razing temples to the ground, destroying the crops standing in the fields and harming the devotees of Vishnu in whatever way they could.

At the same time, the great *asura* declared himself king and decided to go all out and enhance his powers by gaining as many boons as he could.

CHAPTER SIX

LORD VISHNU MAKES A PROMISE

Hiranyakashipu retired to the high mountain called Mandara and began meditating, constantly repeating Lord Brahma's name. He stood on one toe, so that his whole weight rested on it. He raised his arms over his head and placed them together in a yogic pose. His eyes looked up at the sky, and he remained in this position for a long time. Days passed into years, years into decades.

Seeing Hiranyakashipu engaged in such austerities and knowing it would be a long while before Lord Brahma could be appeased, the gods returned to their respective homes relieved. They believed they would be left in peace for a while. Many years passed and Hiranyakashipu did not move an inch. But his devotion and power of concentration were so great that a strange glow began emanating from his head. Soon the glow turned into a blazing ball of fire that spread quickly across the entire universe. Rivers and oceans boiled riotously and tossed up steaming foam that singed

everything it touched. The earth shook and rumbled, and with every crack that appeared on its surface, the blaze only spread further. Very soon the fire spread to other planets and stars.

The gods were now filled with a terrible fear. When all the planets became too hot to live on, and no place offered succour, the gods left their abode in Heaven, for the fire was now licking its walls and threatening to leap over its high gates. They went to meet Lord Brahma and implored him to somehow curtail this terrible heat that swept menacingly out to destroy all that Lord Brahma had created. The gods then disclosed to Lord Brahma Hiranyakashipu's ambition to become immortal and his desire to be the master of the entire universe and everything in it.

Heeding their pleas, Lord Brahma decided to appear before Hiranyakashipu. He flew down on his white swan to where Hiranyakashipu was meditating on Mount Mandara. There, Lord Brahma sprinkled holy water on the *asura* king. At once, the flames subsided and the *asura's* complexion began to shine like gold. When he saw Lord Brahma appear before him, tears of gratitude filled in his eyes.

Lord Brahma was pleased with Hiranyakashipu's devotion. He asked, 'Why have you decided to perform such severe austerities?'

The *asura* bowed low, 'To please you, O Supreme God and Creator, and to ask from you that one gift

that only you as the Creator of the Universe can grant me.'

Brahma understood what he meant. 'Hiranyakashipu, arise. I am pleased with your devotion. Ask for whatever you desire.'

Hiranyakashipu immediately asked for immortality. Brahma refused, explaining that this was a privilege of the gods alone and told the *asura* to ask for something else. Hiranyakashipu looked disappointed. But soon a cunning look came over his eyes and he worded his wish in such a manner that once granted, it would make him near immortal.

Lord Brahma had little choice but to grant the boon. He knew he could not turn the *asura* down a second time as Hiranyakashipu had subjected himself to very harsh conditions just to please him.

Thus having attained great powers, Hiranyakashipu set about harassing every living creature in the universe. The *asura* crossed every boundary in oppression and even raided Heaven on several occasions. He also harassed the sages and holy men. Indra, the King of Gods, was driven to a life on the run. Now, accompanied by the desperate gods, he went to Lord Brahma's abode and prayed for deliverance.

Lord Brahma, who had by now realized the serious implications of his boon, advised the gods to go to Lord Vishnu. If the universe had to be saved from the evil *asura*, only Lord Vishnu could do it. So the gods next trooped to Vaikuntha. Lord Vishnu was also aware of the sufferings caused to many because of Hiranyakashipu's arrogance and his greed for limitless power.

'His time will soon come,' he assured the gods. 'The *asura* has become too arrogant, thinking he can wipe off every god from the face of this universe. But his own pride shall prove to be his downfall. One day he will invite his own destruction, and it is then that I shall appear in my form as Narasimha, the half-man and half-lion.'

The gods trusted Vishnu. After all, he had saved the universe time and again by appearing in different incarnations. And so led by Indra, they went back to the mountains where they had been forced to take shelter since Hiranyakashipu had come to dominate all the realms of the universe.

They were impatient but helpless. However, Lord Vishnu wasn't sitting idle. He knew that a particular moment had been ordained for the avatar that would destroy the great *asura* king. This would be one of his most fearsome avatars and would be a personification of the anger of the god. He prophesied the arrival of Narasimha who would end the tyranny and evil of Hiranyakashipu and restore peace to the world once and for all. But they would have to wait till the time was right for it.

In the meantime, Lord Vishnu, time and again, came to the rescue of his devotees who were being persecuted and killed. And one of the most loyal among them was no other than Hiranyakashipu's son, Prahlada.

CHAPTER SEVEN

PRAHLADA'S SAVIOUR

Prahlada was born when Hiranyakashipu was engaged in the severest of austerities to please Lord Brahma. Taking advantage of Hiranyakashipu's absence, and alarmed by the fire that emanated all around him as his prayers became more and more potent, Lord Indra and the gods attacked Hiranyakashipu's palace.

At this point the divine sage, Narada, intervened to protect Hiranyakashipu's wife, Kayadhu, who was a devout woman, and as pious and virtuous as her husband was evil. Anticipating the attack by the gods, Narada spirited away Kayadhu and her infant son, Prahlada. Kayadhu worshipped Lord Vishnu in secret because Hiranyakashipu would never tolerate Lord

Vishnu being worshipped in the precincts of his own palace. Narada offered her shelter, and his teachings and stories about the miracles and might of Lord Vishnu made a profound impression on the young Prahlada as he grew up. As Prahlada learnt soon, Vishnu was the mightiest of all gods. He was the Preserver, who had saved the earth and the universe time and time again.

When Hiranyakashipu returned more powerful than he had ever been before, the son he had never seen before was already a young boy. As he proceeded to oppress and tyrannize everyone, especially those devoted to Lord Vishnu, it first shocked and then angered him beyond measure to learn that his own son sang Lord Vishnu's praises all the time and swore an undying devotion to him.

His fury towards his son knew no bounds because he had issued the strictest orders that Lord Vishnu would not be worshipped anywhere in his realm. His *asura* soldiers had destroyed all idols and temples that were dedicated to Vishnu, and priests of such temples and the god's ardent worshippers had been dragged away, humiliated and imprisoned. However, his father's taunts, threats and humiliations had no impact on Prahlada. He continued to worship Lord Vishnu, and met his mother in secret to hear the oft-repeated stories about the great god.

Hiranyakashipu's advisers carried tales of Prahlada's devotion and complete dedication to Lord Vishnu back to their master. Hiranyakashipu was so upset at hearing these stories that his face turned red. His flaming golden hair flew about his face as he raved and ranted. He then tore his hair out in frustration, and in the end he came to a most awful and evil decision. He decided to kill his own son as an example for all of Lord Vishnu's devotees.

Hiranyakashipu first instructed his advisers to have Prahlada thrown into the river, with a stone tied to his legs so that he would sink to the bottom. The soldiers left him struggling in the river, but to everyone's amazement, Prahlada returned to the palace unscathed and unhurt. He had no memory of how he came to be in the palace and thought it had all been a dream. But what had actually happened was that Lord Vishnu had appeared and untied the boulder tied to his legs. He had then carried him safely back to the river bank.

Hiranyakashipu was undaunted by this failure. He did not give up his attempts, though Kayadhu pleaded with him to spare their son's life. Hiranyakashipu had Prahlada captured, placed in chains and thrown at the feet of the wildest elephant in his stables, so that he could be trampled to death. No one in the kingdom protested as Prahlada, bound and chained, was laid out before the elephant. But a strange thing happened. The elephant that had been running amok all this while, came to a thundering stop when he saw the small boy lying helpless on the ground before him. Then he

lowered his head, and placing his trunk lovingly around Prahlada, lifted him and put him on his own back.

Next, Hiranyakashipu tried to poison Prahlada, but Vishnu appeared and drank up the poison in secret. Thus every attempt to kill this brave little boy was thwarted by Lord Vishnu and this made the *asura* king even angrier and more determined to kill him.

CHAPTER EIGHT

ON THE BURNING PYRE

Hiranyakashipu refused to give up or to believe that Lord Vishnu could have worked a miracle to save his devotee. One of Hiranyakashipu's most dastardly attempts to kill his son was by making him sit on a burning pyre with his sister Holika. Holika had special powers that prevented her from ever being harmed by fire and according to the plan, she would hold him tight until he burnt to a cinder.

Prahlada was led to a gigantic pyre with Holika sitting at the absolute pinnacle. Yet, he was not afraid.

He chanted Lord Vishnu's name to himself, as Holika cradled him and the flames of fire rose higher and higher around them. Yet, not a hair on his head was harmed; instead it was his aunt, Holika, who perished in the fire. This burning of Holika is celebrated on the eve of the festival of Holi. It is believed that Lord Vishnu stepped in to protect Prahlada and Holika burnt instead.

However, the reason Holika perished was that she had been given her miraculous power by Lord Brahma on the understanding that she would never use it to harm anyone. Since she had chosen to obey her wicked brother Hiranyakashipu's command to end Prahlada's life, the fire destroyed her instead.

Another story says that Holika was actually a good person but was forced to listen to her brother. When she sat in the fire holding Prahlada, the clothes she wore protected her from fire. However, knowing that what was happening was wrong, and that Prahlada was in grave danger, she gave her protective cloak to Prahlada and chose to die herself.

Yet another story mentions that the shawl that Holika wore was to protect her from fire. So when she was asked to sit in the fire with Prahlada, she put on the shawl and placed Prahlada in her lap. When the fire was lit, Prahlada began praying fervently to Lord Vishnu. And Lord Vishnu, heeding the call of his devotee, summoned a gust of wind to blow the shawl off Holika and onto Prahlada, saving him from the flames and burning Holika to death.

Whatever be the story, Holika died, and not a hair

on Prahlada's head was harmed. Yet, the generals of Hiranyakashipu refused to give up. They struck Prahlada with sharp weapons and forced the young boy into life-threatening situations; but each time they were unsuccessful.

Meanwhile, the sons of Shukracharya, who was the guru of all the *asuras*, began tutoring Prahlada in the way of the *asuras*, but Prahlada refused to accept their knowledge, knowing that what they preached was evil. When the teachers were absent from the classroom, Prahlada began teaching the other *asura* students about the virtues and goodness of Lord Vishnu, and in no time most of the young *asura* boys were enamoured of the god.

These sons of Shukracharya were known as Chanda and Amarka. Although they were knowledgable and wise, they were afraid of Hiranyakashipu's wrath. Once they saw Prahlada teaching the young *asuras* and they became afraid that the other students would get influenced by the boy and become devoted to Lord Vishnu. So, they informed Hiranyakashipu about what Prahlada was up to. This made him really angry and now he was resolved more than ever before to destroy his son and challenge Lord Vishnu.

It was then that Lord Vishnu knew he could put things off no more and that the time was now imminent for Narasimha to appear. This had been foretold by a heavenly prophecy when Jaya and Vijaya were cursed by the Kumaras. Lord Vishnu had promised that he would appear in each of their births in a new avatar and help ease their pain. As this particular avatar was that of a very powerful *asura*, Lord Vishnu also had to take on an equally fierce form to defeat him.

The fearsome Narasimha emerged from a shattered pillar and crushed Hiranyakashipu, thereby freeing him from his curse and protecting his greatest devotee, Prahlada, with a single divine blow.

MythNotes

It is believed that the gods feared Narasimha's wrath so much that they went to Lord Shiva to beg him to temper the creature's rage. It was then that Shiva assumed the form of Sharaba, an eight-legged bird, with the face of a lion. Sharaba's form was even more unusual and terrifying than that of Narasimha. In a duel between these two very strange creatures, it was Narasimha who had to accept defeat. By accepting Sharaba as his superior, he acknowledged the power of Shiva. As Narasimha merged himself in Sharaba and lost his ferocity, it reflected a symbolic union between the powers of two of the mightiest gods in the universe, Shiva the Destroyer, and Vishnu the Preserver.

In the Sri Lakshminarasimha Swamy temple in Nalgonda district in Andhra Pradesh, Lord Narasimha is believed to be a great healer and is known as 'Vaidya Narasimha' by his devotees. He is believed to have the power to cure diseases and save those who are under the influence of witchcraft and black magic. People in this area believe that Narasimha appears in dreams, administers medicines and even operates on patients, and they wake up cured of their ailments.

Narasimha is one of the most popular religious icons in the art and sculpture of south India. A famous example is the giant Ugra Narasimha statue in Hampi, Karnataka.